W9-APJ-359

Forgiveness
The Key
to the Kingdom

Books by John-Roger

Awakening Into Light
Baraka
Blessings of Light
Buddha Consciousness
The Christ Within & The Disciples of Christ
  with the Cosmic Christ Calendar
The Consciousness of Soul
A Consciousness of Wealth
Dream Voyages
Drugs
Dynamics of the Lower Self
Forgiveness: The Key to the Kingdom
God Is Your Partner
Inner Worlds of Meditation
The Journey of a Soul
Loving...Each Day
Manual on Using the Light
The Master Chohans of the Color Rays
Passage Into Spirit
The Path to Mastership
Possessions, Projections & Entities
The Power Within You
Psychic Protection
Q&A Journal from the Heart
Relationships: The Art of Making Life Work
Sex, Spirit & You
The Signs of the Times
The Sound Current
The Spiritual Family
The Spiritual Promise
Spiritual Warrior: The Art of Spiritual Living
The Tao of Spirit
Walking with the Lord
The Way Out Book
Wealth & Higher Consciousness

For further information, please contact:

MSIA⁽ᵉ⁾
P.O. Box 513935,
Los Angeles, CA 90051-1935
(323) 737-4055
soul@msia.org
www.msia.org
www.forgive.org

JOHN-ROGER

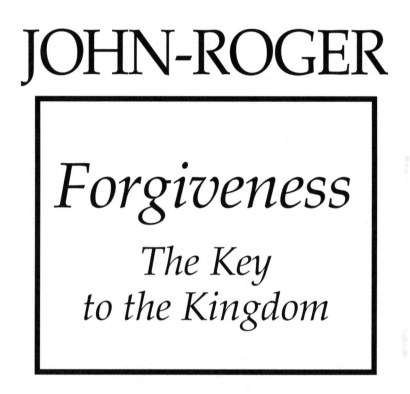

Forgiveness

The Key
to the Kingdom

With a Foreword by John Morton

MANDEVILLE PRESS
Los Angeles, California

Copyright 1994, 1999
Peace Theological Seminary
& College of Philosophy"

All rights reserved,
including the right of reproduction
in whole or in part in any form.

Published by Mandeville Press
P.O. Box 513935
Los Angeles, CA 90051-1935
e-mail: jrbooks@msia.org

Visit us on the Web at www.forgive.org

Printed in the United States of America
I.S.B.N. 0-914829-62-9

"Peter came to Jesus and asked,
 'Lord, how many times
 shall I forgive my brother
 when he sins against me?
 Up to seven times?'

"Jesus answered,
 'I tell you, not seven times,
 but seventy-seven times.'"

Matthew 18:21-22 NIV

*"Do not judge,
and you will not be judged.*

*Do not condemn,
and you will not be condemned.*

Forgive, and you will be forgiven."

Luke 6:37 NIV

"Jesus said,
'Father, forgive them,
for they do not know
what they are doing.'"

Luke 23:34 NIV

Foreword

In a world in which we find so much pain, violence, injustice, and strife, a resolution is dearly needed. Forgiveness, *although always available,* is so often disregarded or not even considered.

Forgiveness heals the wounds from the past that cannot be changed, cleansing that which would fester, sealing that which must be set to rest.

Contrary to what many believe, forgiveness does not absolve people of responsibility or allow misdeeds to perpetuate. Rather, it frees God's blessings from the clutches of anguish and condemnation. We must forgive our misdeeds that misrepresent and mislead so that we may remember that the best is yet to come.

John-Roger, with his depth of humanity and compassionate wisdom, elucidates how forgiveness unlocks the imprisoned heart. With simplicity, every passage on every page guides us from not knowing how to be free to the love that overcomes all. Forgiveness: the key to living in grace.

JOHN MORTON

October, 1998

Introduction

Forgiving ourselves certainly seems to go against the grain of our human conditioning. Even the idea can bring up feelings of unworthiness or skepticism that it could possibly work. Yet if we recognize that we are, indeed, divine beings made in God's image, the idea does not seem too far-fetched, and as we look at life from that higher perspective, the idea of holding on to judgments and seeking revenge or retribution begins to seem the far odder approach.

This book is designed to point us back to ourselves as sacred, spiritual beings who have been given the gift of creation. We can use this gift to create positively or negatively. Often, when we see our negative creation or its consequences—for example, when we have gotten angry and have hurt the feelings of someone we love—it is easy to feel bad and to judge our action and ourselves. Unfortunately, that type of approach only compounds the negativity.

Punishing ourselves in an attempt to balance the action through the law of "an eye for an eye and a tooth for a tooth" is a lower path. Forgiveness is the higher road. It is the road on which we walk under grace. And it is this road that has been prepared for us by the great spiritual masters who have come forward and demonstrated the consciousness of the Christ.

How, then, do you forgive yourself? The first thing you can do is simply say, "I forgive myself." Then, just let go of what is bothering you. If you wish, you can add, "I let this go into the Light, for the highest good," or "I give this to God."

How do you know if you have really let it go? You may find yourself taking a deep breath, you may experience a lightness, or you may just feel better inside. Then again, you may feel nothing at all. This does not mean that nothing has happened; however, if you still sense the presence of the imbalance or negativity, it could be that you need to be more specific or precise in your forgiveness.

For example, you can say, "I forgive myself for judging my father for not giving me the love I wanted," or "I forgive myself for judging myself for not feeling worthy of my parents' love." Feel free to keep trying out lots of possibilities, and it really helps to be sincere, honest, and direct with yourself.

Notice that each phrase starts with "I forgive myself." This is because we are taking responsibility for the negativity or imbalance we have been holding on to. We can say that we forgive the other person, but, in reality, they have already been forgiven by God, so it isn't necessary. God has already forgiven us, too, but if we are still carrying the weight of the negativity, it is then necessary to forgive ourselves.

Even though the person we have judged may no longer be in our lives, or may even be dead, we still may be carrying them inside ourselves as less than the divine being they are. So it is inside that we must bring ourselves to peace with them, and forgiveness is one of the most effective ways of doing that.

Before going to sleep at night, it is nice to quickly review the day and forgive yourself for anything that is still on your mind or troubling you. And you can also do this throughout the day, whenever you notice yourself judging, so that, as J-R has said, you live in a constant state of forgiveness.

Sometimes, however, we don't want to forgive ourselves, or we are so cut off from our loving that we don't know where to start. When this happens to me, I come back to the following words of John-Roger to get me back on track: "The basic thing we need to do is to forgive ourselves for forgetting that we are divine. That is the real message to open up the channel for our return to the Spirit."

John-Roger has often said that God is in the business of forgiveness. As I have looked at life on this planet, I have often thought that perhaps our job is to make sure that God stays in business. Then again, perhaps God put us here because He wanted His children to get the necessary training so that they could go into His business.

Paul Kaye

Forgiveness

The Key
to the Kingdom

The Coin in Your Purse

A person once came up to Jesus and said, "Look at all the terrible things these people have done to you. Lord, let's pay them back."

And Jesus said, "I have to pay them back with the coin I have in my purse." What was that? Love and forgiveness.

Wouldn't it be nice if that's the coin you have in your heart? Love and forgiveness. Do you know what forgiveness really entails? Repenting from your judgment, forgetting that you made the judgment, and living your life from that point on.

And if you make a mistake, learn from it. You can beat yourself up, but listen: when you are down, one thing you don't need is somebody to step on your face. When you're down, you don't need somebody to say how terrible you looked when you fell.

What is it you need when you're down? A helping hand. You need good thoughts inside of you to counterbalance the bad thoughts. And you'd better have an arsenal of affirmations that can pick you up out of any situation and straighten you out and get you going.

Live Your Life the
Best You Can

*L*ive your life the best that you can. It can be hard, even on good days, but still do it, and work the best you can and give yourself credit.

And if you have flaws, fine. Just don't focus on them; work on them. If you looked only at your flaws, you probably wouldn't feel worthy to be here because you would see the errors of your behavior and the imperfections of your body. So focus on the goodness of the work you do, and then correct the flaws as you go along.

The negative thinking that we can hold inside ourselves is really a demonstration of great mind power. What would happen if we decided to move that to a positive action and go for the essence behind all our actions as being that which is loving, caring, and sharing, and health, wealth, and happiness, and prosperity, abundance, and riches for everyone? And inside, we are doing Soul transcendence, and when we're not, we're loving, caring, and sharing.

Looking Through Grace

*G*race is God's formless form,
or the essence.

Behind everyone who is negative is a
crying out for love and understanding.
Behind every accusation is a cry for help.

If we look through grace, we look at
supplying the wherewithal for the person to
move out of their imprisonment, which is
the law, into the formless, which is their
living, loving, caring, and sharing of the
beauty and the gratefulness of life.

That includes God in all of its wisdom,
all of its infiniteness, all of its compassion,
and all of its sustaining us through the
negative and the positive aspects of our life.

Christ Is Forgiveness

*W*e have to understand that all of us have very similar reactions to the environment of this world, and in that we can give compassion to people. In that compassion, we enter into grace.

Christ is forgiveness. Love is forgiving. Love is for the giving. God gives all the time. If we're going to enter into God, what is it we must start doing? Giving all the time.

We then become commutators of divine energy into this world, and the kingdom of heaven appears in us, around us, as us. And all the things we want come to us in the way that is noble and honorable, for the best of us and for the worst of us. And those are all the same things because there is no better or worse when we're in this dimension of Spirit. For in that height, we see that everything we've done that's been a yea or a nay or a good or a bad or a judgment or an evil has been a progression in learning, a karmic fulfillment, a debt paid, a new, life-giving experience to someone else.

Christ Is Forgiveness

continued

So we start to rejoice in the wondrousness that we're part of a creation that is our own, that a God creator-form, of which we're an extension, has that type of magnificence, knows all of us by our name, and recognizes us as the Divinity. And in that, we have our coming and our going.

I've never found a place where God was not already there. Even when I didn't recognize it, He was there. It was my perception that needed correcting, not God's.

Being in God's Will

*T*he neat thing to know is that the law of God is just and it's impartial. Yet some of you may say that God should give you a break. If you enter into the grace of *now*, God gives you the break. So all the breaks are in our hands and our control.

It's really nice to know that we're controlling our future in the sense that we come under the Divine guidance and make our will one with God's will. It doesn't take anything away from us; we don't lose individuality, we don't lose respect, we don't lose anything.

We can still go out, get drunk, fall in the ditch, and still be in God's will, because nothing is taken away from us. We just know that what we're doing is part of the Divine plan. When we are outside of knowing it's part of the Divine plan, we get drunk and fall, and we think we're a dirty alcoholic. Or if we see somebody else do that, we say, "What a terrible person. They ought to go to hell or be locked up."

Being in God's Will

continued

But when we come back into God's will, we say, "I can see this. This is your last lifetime, and you're fighting off the negativity this way. Let me help you up." And then we become not do-gooders, but people who are just doing the goodness.

Enlightenment

*Y*ou can ask, "How would Christ handle this situation that I am in?" You put on the eyes of the Christ; you look through them and say, "Well, Christ would do this." Then you do that. And that is the enlightenment.

If I declare to you that I am enlightened and there are no criteria by which you can see that, then I can also declare to you that I'm a billionaire and use the same criteria for you not to know that, either. So there must be an empirical, objective point by which you look at enlightenment.

Enlightenment is not a bright light that shines and blinds everybody. That's called blinding everybody. Enlightenment is the process by which you relate to people in your conversation, in your daily occupation. And one of the foremost things to look for in enlightenment is forgiveness.

When you go into a situation with some-one, you should have an anchor into the Spirit of who you are so you can come back out of it. And the way in is the way out. So if you think step by step into judgment, you must think step by step back out into forgiveness. In the judgment is the "endarkenment," and in the forgiveness is the enlightenment.

The Forgiving Father

*D*o you remember the story of the prodigal son, who left his dad, took half his inheritance and squandered it, and went into endarkenment?

The son said, "Even to live in my father's house as a low servant is better than to live where I am now," and so he began to return home. On the way back home, he got more and more excited about being there. And when he got home, his father saw him coming and shined his enlightenment upon his son; the father went out and fell on his son, kissing him on the neck and bringing him back in.

The son who stayed home started going into endarkenment, saying, "Why are you doing this to my brother, who took half of his things and went off to squander them, and I stayed and worked with you?"

The father said, "Because he's come home, and all he's done is forgiven. And to you, son, all that I have is already yours."

What the father didn't say is, "And don't blow it by judging your brother. He's got a lot of wounds to be healed. He needs a lot of nurturing and caring."

That's a story of enlightenment.

Moving into the
Field of Battle

*W*e have an opportunity to participate in our life as a statement of loving and caring and sharing and nurturing. Not climbing up on the mountain and staying in safety, but actually moving down into the field of battle. Not fighting, but forgiving the fighting.

One Accord

The keynote of everything we do is to be of one accord. Prior to the one accord, there is discussion. Once the thing discussed is agreed upon and we've made a loving commitment to it, we move.

Then, when you talk and do things, you find that people will start to assist you. You feel grateful for that, but you won't really feel the gratitude until someone else asks for help and you do help them. Then you feel the gratitude of the giving and the joy that comes with freely giving.

Be Grateful

*I*t's really important to realize that the attitude you hold is the attitude that brings to you what's present in your life.

If things in your life are not coming down the way you want them to, change your attitude and be grateful that you get what you get that's coming down.

God Doesn't See Evil

$\mathcal{W}$e come under grace when we're willing to listen and look at the face of God, wherever that is showing.

This is not easy to do. It's a very difficult thing to do because the habits of this world are very, very powerful.

If you die in your "evil," who's to handle it? It's yours. The only thing you can do to balance that is to come back again. But what if you come back with less remembrance than you had before and with a body wanting to contract itself and a mind and emotions wanting to protect themselves from all the horrendous things you've done? Having no memory, you do more evil.

Finally, you walk up to somebody who says, "There's no good reason to ever withdraw your loving." And so you look at the evil you do and you love it, and it is changed to good. That's why God doesn't see evil, because His goodness transforms it.

What Is Forgiveness?

Q: What is the true meaning of forgiveness? When I say, "I forgive," what am I saying?

A: If you ever had your feelings hurt and you forgave the person for it, and, inside of you, you allowed them the chance to hurt your feelings again, then you really did forgive them.

You entered into real, true forgiveness because you allowed them the opportunity to come back to you again. That's forgiveness. But if you remember who they were and what they said and what they did and the time they did it, and if you say you forgave them, you didn't.

We don't really forgive when we still have the feeling of the memory of the hurt.

What to Pray For

*S*o, what are you going to pray for?

If your answer is, "I'm going to pray for all these things that I want," you had better think about it because the scripture says, "Even before you pray, God knows what you want and is delivering it to you."

Does that mean we're invalidating prayer? No. But I have my own radical approach. I get on my hands and knees, and I say, "Dear God, I don't want anything from you, but I'd like to know what it is you want from me. Would you let me know what you want? Because that's the difficulty I may be having—finding out what it is you're giving me that I'm missing."

Sure, it's a little radical, but have you ever stopped to think about it? If God is already supplying everything, before I even ask, why am I missing so much? It's because I was so busy asking that it was going by me.

I should have said, "Open my eyes so I may see." That's the prayer, right there.

It's very simple, all day long: "God, what is it you want from me?"

Forgive Yourself

*E*verything everybody has ever said they've done—I've already done it.

I forgive myself first, for doing something that would make me forgive myself.

Innocence

*W*hen we have really forgiven somebody, we enter into original innocence. And that original innocence is like new snow. It's like fresh rain that clears the air.

It's anything where you just go, "Wow." I guess it's every sunset I've ever seen.... They're all new.

Grieving

Grieving is a working out of the blockage of the emotions and the mind.

Sometimes it's crying that does it.

Sometimes fasting does it.

Sometimes running does it.

Sometimes hard work will do it.

There are a lot of things that do it. But to *do* it is very important.

Awakening to the Divine

*W*hatever you need to forgive in another person, do it, because it's important to restore that person to the original image that brought you into relationship with them in the first place.

It's called, love, kindness, and consideration.

You restore their image inside of you, and then you attempt to help them restore the image inside of them. In other words, we help each one awaken to the presence of the Divine inside of them. Then Divinity speaks. And that's us, not singularly, but collectively.

Talk About It

*I*s there someone you cannot forgive? Is there something that people do that you cannot forgive? Why do you hate them? It's because you can't forgive them.

What did they do?

"They hurt my feelings."

Where did you have your feelings?

"Well, right here on my sleeve. I took my heart and put it out here, and I said, 'Here, love me.'"

Yes, and they said, "Excuse me," as they bumped into you.

And you said, "Why are you doing that to me? All I wanted was love."

Well, you had your heart in the way and on your sleeve. And if you ask them what happened, they'll probably say, "I wasn't trying to hurt you. I just wanted your arm moved so I could put my arm around you, and it hit on the way up."

Talk About It

continued

"Oh, you mean that you were making an effort to hug me, and when you hit me in the chin, you didn't mean it? Oh, good. Now I can forgive that."

Why? Because you talked about it with that other person. And you understand that it was really just a mistake.

The Lord Is
Always Available

I've been under the impression (and I have my experience for it) that the Lord has always been available. And I also have to admit that I wasn't always available to the Lord's availability.

When I finally came to that conclusion, it was then a matter of my moving back to the position of being with the Lord. I then realized that the Lord never moved because the Lord didn't really know how to move. He only knew how to be with me all the time. It was a remarkable thing to find out that he knew that more than he knew anything else.

Then when I found that the Lord knew it with others, well, it got to be really tremendous inside of me. In fact, my ego trip left real fast. I said, "This Lord knows how to be with everybody all the time, so I don't suppose there are any restrictions, though I had placed restrictions."

And whenever I turn to that, there it is. There it is. There it is.

Enlightening Yourself

That moment inside of you where you forgive what's happened is the moment when you are enlightening yourself.

Making the Most
Out of a Situation

*S*ometimes the best way to make the most out of a situation is to get out of it. The other way is to accept it and be grateful that it isn't worse.

I find that it's much easier to just love it all. When it shows up, I go, "Wow. Another form of loving. Another face of loving. Another expression of loving. Another location of loving." And then I get to participate in it.

That's grateful.

Grace Is Loving God

$\mathcal{T}$he only grace is loving God.

If you want grace, you love God, and *then* you get it. And when you don't get grace, you're not loving God.

Your approach has probably been to want to get grace first, and then you'll love God. It doesn't work that way. I wish it did. I wish I could see the kingdom of heaven first, and then repent.

On My Way to
See Who Forgave Me

A man once said to me, "Do you understand that when I accepted Christ as my personal savior, I was forgiven?"

And I said, "That's wonderful, but did you forget all your sins?"

"No."

"Then," I said, "you must forgive yourself by forgetting and coming into the presence of Light and love and laughter and joy."

He asked me, "What do *you* do?"

So I told him, "I may be forgiven, but I'm on my way to see who forgave me. I don't have time to look at the shadows that are being cast by the bright Light that shines upon me."

Seeing the Face of God

*H*ow on earth do you gain forgiveness when you've forgiven yourself and the stuff keeps coming back up?

I know that we all have very similar feelings that stop us from moving forward into what we really want. We have to address with courage, conviction, and all the willpower that we have whatever it is that stands in the way.

It takes great courage to see the face of God, because you first have to look at your own.

An Ultimate Selfishness

*I*f I'm going to do something that will make me need to forgive myself, I don't do it. Because that's putting it against myself to start with. And if you're going to do something to me, where I'll have to forgive you, I'm not going to let you do that. This is, in a sense, an ultimate selfishness.

I'm going to take care of myself so well that when you're around me, you'll be able to do whatever you want to do without worrying about me, because if you do something that I don't want you to do around me, I'll tell you.

It's an ultimate selfishness, but do you understand it's also unconditional loving? Because that way, you're free. And when you're free, the Spirit comes forward, which is what I really want to see in people anyway— the Spirit.

Forget It

*Y*ou don't get forgiveness until you forget what it is that is blocking you.

Living Your Life
to Completeness

*I*f I'm going to have forgiveness, who am I going to have it from? Myself. But every time I forgive myself for something, I'm remembering what it was. And every time I remember what it was, I put some more of my energy into it. So it seems to get bigger and doesn't go away.

So although I say, "Okay, I forgive myself," the next time I see the person that I got angry with, up comes the anger again.

So we have to do something more than forgive it. We actually have to forget it. We have to live our lives in this moment to such completeness that when one moment disappears, there's no evidence that we were in that moment.

If there's no evidence, there'll be no thought, no feeling, no imagination, and no physical reality, and the unconscious will be clear.

Living Your Life
to Completeness

continued

Do you know what happens when those levels clear themselves? We automatically move very deep inside ourselves into the Soul, wherein the Christ and God, the divine spiritual energy, the Holy Spirit, the Holy Ghost, resides and lives.

Keep Your Focus on God

*T*he scriptures tell us the Lord said that he "will remember their sins no more." When you don't remember, you have forgotten, and in the forgetting, you are forgiven. You are fore-given.

So something new is coming into you, and it will occupy the space that greeds and guilts formerly occupied. They were draining your vitality and your life. They're negativity-producing and negativity-attracting. And they're going to pull to you what you focus upon, what you don't want.

Do you remember these statements?
Your fears are upon you.
What you fear, you get.
What goes around, comes around.
Reincarnation.

All of that is saying, do not focus on anything but God.

The Most
Important Thing

*W*hat's the hardest thing we have to do as people who are following Christ, people who are following God, people who are following love? We've got to be forgiving. That's the most important thing we've got to do.

Then people come up and start running the law on you. If you forgive them and they hit you, what do you do? Forgive them. What if they hit you again? Forgive them. What if they do it again? Don't be stupid—get out of reach. And forgive them again.

Immaturity

You probably don't remember what you did on the third day in the second grade of school because it's done, it's over, it's complete. But if you remember Mrs. Jones in the fourth grade and the time she slapped you, you'd better start forgetting that one, also, because you've got some immaturity working that's going to block you. And that immaturity of a fourth-grade level may start running your life.

You may say, "Well, my dad hurt me when I was thirteen." You've got a thirteen-year-old running a fifty-year-old man. You had better get that thirteen-year-old up to date.

You can clean it out by just not focusing on that again. And you can clean it out by moving into the Soul. Be sure to bury it deep enough that it gets to the *Soul*. If you don't (and many people have stopped very short of getting there), you put it into the unconscious, and then you run yourself from a habitual pattern of unconsciousness, and you may have to seek out psychotherapy. Then you've got to go relive it and be responsible and accountable for all those past things, and that's not necessary.

Immaturity

continued

You don't have to do that. Why? Because we are creators in the exact perfect image of God in the Spirit, and we can dissolve it. We can dissolve it by a dismissal, by not putting our energy on it any more.

Love It

*H*ow about loving what you do?

"No, I can't. I just told somebody off out of emotional upset."

Great. Love it.

"I can't love it."

Forget it.

"I can't forget it."

Go back and apologize.

"Well, that means I have to be accountable for it."

Yes, that's the other way.

"Okay, I'll forget it."

Keep in Mind
Your Purpose

To receive, you must be active. Keep in mind your purpose. You will receive in direct proportion to your clarity of vision, your definiteness of purpose, the steadiness of your faith, and the depth of your gratitude.

Look for the Blessing

*E*ven in the midst of the curse, the blessing appears.

Sometimes we've desired something and didn't get it, and we've cussed God, our wives, our husbands, our lousy kids, and everybody else in the world—and then weeks later the better thing comes forward. Then we don't know what to do because we've put God down, we've put our wife or husband down, we've put the kids down, we've put everybody down, but here comes this wonderful opportunity.

It's because Spirit, the substance of life, had the better one coming for you and negated the one that was not going to give you the fullness that you had tuned in to. And so it looked like a curse, but the blessing was right behind it.

A State of Competition

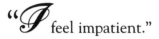

"*I* feel impatient."

Be grateful for what you've got right now.

"Well, I have this next breath of air."

Where did the impatience go?

"Oh. I forgot about it because I felt gratitude for the breath of air."

That's what I'm talking about. Feel gratitude for the person next to you. You find out that this is an easier, nicer way to live than trying to beat somebody out of something, to get ahead of them and compete.

Every time you're in a hurry to finish and go to the next thing, you're in a state of competition, and negativity is going to result from it.

Every time you're in a state of gratitude and have clarity of vision and are making the leap of faith into it by walking toward it, you're producing the positive energy around you. Then people will look at you, and you'll wonder why they're staring. It's because they are seeing a demonstration of that invisible substance being made visible.

The Hand of
Enlightenment

*A*s you change behavior, you change the emotion. As you change the emotion, you change the thinking. As you change the thinking, you're getting wisdom. As you gain wisdom, you go into forgiveness.

You forgive yourself your own stupidity and ignorance and lack of knowledge, and you forgive everybody else in the same instant. And at that moment, you're moving into enlightenment.

Not only do you say, "I forgive you," but you also forgive as a process of beingness.

Your attitude is one where you would reach down into the muck and mire of where someone is and gently lift them out and cleanse them from what they had on them, as bad and terrible as it may be.

The Hand of
Enlightenment

continued

That reaching into the muck and the mire to meet somebody where they are and to pull them back out into the Light—that will look like you've gone into darkness. And the one you pull out, who has all that junk all over them, will look at your hand and think you're as junky as they are. But as they get cleaned up—and that process is theirs—they will see that you've also got a very clean hand of enlightenment. That's a very, very important challenge for human beings.

Maintain Contact
with the Loving

*G*race is God's righteousness, where "when you do it to the least one of these, you've done it unto me," and "love God with your body, mind, and Soul and your neighbor as yourself."

Those who are under the law are not loving themselves. The Bible says, "A man who lacks judgment derides his neighbor, but a man of understanding holds his tongue." Do you understand that? We stop finding faults in people, and we start to understand that what they're going through is their process, and we just let them do it. It's called, "That's their '10-percent level,' their own area of concern."

People don't hook me into their 10 percent because I don't buy into it. I might listen to it, and I still always maintain my own independent thought and my own independent feeling and the contact with the loving that is always present.

Don't Look for Perfection

*D*o yourself a big favor and don't look for perfection here.

If I could say, "God, grant them one wish," it would be, "Grant them that they will make the best use that they can muster of what comes their way. And then go on."

The Moment
Before Death

*I*f we don't know the moment we're going to die, so that we can forgive ourselves and chant God's holy name just before we die, we might want to chant all the time.

Peace, Be Still

The physical world will always be a reflection. The inner world will always be reality.

At the point where we bring the inner world out, the veil of the flesh falls on us, and we become entrapped by our responses to other people's bodies, thoughts, and consciousnesses, and then we're confused. "Harry said this, Susie said that, Mary's doing this, Joe said, 'Don't do that.' What shall I do?"

Stop listening to them. They're adding insult to your injury.

Take yourself to a quiet spot. If it can be physically quiet, that would be beautiful. Often a good, quiet spot is in front of a picture on a wall that can help you enhance your attunement. And when you do this, you can say, "Peace, be still," and it will happen to you.

Peace, Be Still

continued

The emotions will subside, the mind will quiet, and you can simply add, "Lord, I receive."

It's very sacred when we can say in our consciousness, "Lord, I receive right now whatever it is that you're bestowing upon me. You can touch it to me now, at this moment."

What's My Work Here?

*W*hat is the work that you're here to do?

The most immediate thing in front of you.

Called what?

Called two choices. Either live under the law of karma or live under God's grace of loving. You can have your choice.

And the grace of God did not say for one minute that you won't have any pain. It just said you are going to live in the Spirit while you walk through this world.

A Tale of the Healing
of Memories

*A*ll too often we want to take the things that our parents did to us when we were youngsters and use them against ourselves. We'll say that "my mother made me this way" or "my father made me that way." I'm not saying it is or isn't true. But, you know, I tried that on my father once.

We were way up in the high mountains of Utah, riding in a truck, and I was the one driving. That was pretty unusual because my dad didn't usually let anybody else drive him in a truck high up in the mountains on narrow roads with 10,000-foot drops down the side.

I figured that was a good time to ask him a question because he wouldn't hit me or yell at me because I might jerk and go off the road. I figured that he'd have to play it cool. I had my timing down really well; I had about a five-mile stretch over a really bad road where we couldn't go too fast even though we were going downhill. I told him why I thought something had happened wrong in my life because of Mother and him.

My dad said, "Wait a minute," and my foot went on the brake. I thought, "Oh, I shouldn't

A Tale of the Healing
of Memories

continued

have done that. I should've kept going but just waited a minute inside." But I stopped.

He looked at me and said, "Son, for people who are ignorant, that might really be true, but you're intelligent, you have a college education, and you have the wit to know that anything that happened to you as a child and when you were going through school most likely happened all right. And you're smart enough not to let that bother you from now on, either between you inside of you, or between you and me or your mother. Let's go." And I went down the road.

You know something? He was right. If I had gone on and promoted that, that would've been so. But he just told me, "You don't lay these things against me and your mother. We did the best we knew how with what we were doing. And you're smart enough now that you can see and make up any mistake that we made."

My dad healed a memory in me. And the healing of memories is one of the most vital ministries that the Traveler has.

Simple Directions for
Living Life

*Y*our mind will say things to you, and then your eyes will start to look around for whatever it is that your mind says you lack. Then your emotions start to follow that, the feelings start to hurt, the body grabs a hold of it, and pretty soon you're sick.

So now you know how to be sick, and you know how to make yourself even sicker. Yet you can reverse that. You do it by watching where you put your eyes. Watch what you hold in your mind. Watch where you put the feelings as they come up. Put your emotions where you want your body to go. These are very simple directions for just living life.

Spiritual Exercises

*T*hose who are doing the spiritual exercises stop functioning under the law and come under grace, and the grace is given freely.

You might say, "I really am paying something for it. I'm doing the spiritual exercises."

Yes, and you keep breathing, too. You pay for that, also, but it is free.

We're in God's Hands

*I*n the Garden of Gethsemane, Jesus gave us a picture of gratitude when he said, "Nevertheless, your will be done."

And the gratitude of that statement was that there was a Father who had all things in His hand and that even Jesus was in that hand.

God Is in the

Forgiving Business

More and more, the things on this planet are being pulled out from under us to make us stop relying upon that which has never been reliable, that which can never provide security. This places us in the only thing that is secure and that does not disappear: that which exists, that which is, that which is never born and never dies, that which is who you truly are.

Who you truly are is the truthsayer, and it will say it over and over and over, as long as it takes, until each one of us knows that. The nice thing is (and this is both the good news and the bad news), it will give you as many opportunities as you need.

If you think all is lost and that you are not going to make it, I'd like to remind you of one thing about God and that's this: God is in the forgiving business.

All These Catastrophes

*L*ook at all the times in your past when you have had doubt and fear and you said, "Oh, God, how am I getting through this? I'll never make it through."

Then you look in the mirror, and it says, "Liar," because you lied to yourself. You said you couldn't make it or you never would make it, and there you are as living proof that you were wrong.

This, then, should tell you that you are making it, over and over and over, through all these catastrophes that are in your head. You're making it, and you continue to make it, so why be concerned by the next one?

Thank God

Thank God I'm doing this now instead of later, when I might not be able to do it.

Thank God I got trashed today instead of next week, when it's going to be important.

Thank God they beat me up today, so I'm stronger for next week.

Thank God this opportunity came in right now, when I'm ready for it.

And thank God I didn't handle it worse than I did.

All that is just an attitude of gratitude.

Next

*P*eople may come up to you and say, "You dirty, rotten so-and-so," and all you need to say is, "What else?"

They may say, "Is that it?"

You say, "Yep. Next."

"Why?"

"Forget it. Next."

"Well, what I said is important."

"No, it isn't. Next."

"But what I feel is . . ."

"Forget it. Next."

"But I think . . ."

"Forget that one. Next."

"Well, but what I saw in my mind was . . ."

"Next."

"Well, I have this thing inside of me that compulsively . . ."

"Forget it. Next."

"That just leaves me."

"Ah, wonderful. Marvelous. You. The most important person in the world. And that 'you' is everybody."

Appreciate
Your Negativity

I think you should learn to appreciate your irritation, appreciate your negativity. Then you end up, no matter what happens, as quite an appreciative person.

It may seem foolish, but another word for that would be gratefulness, that you are being a grateful person. And this grateful feeling has a very strange quality about it that says, "I won't let in anything else that is not grateful."

The more that feeling of grateful appears, the more it holds out everything else that is not that and allows the grateful in. At the same time, you will be transmuting your karma through the inner traveling, which is the way it's going to work anyway.

Go for Excellence

The best way to deal with shame is to own that it's part of the human condition to have shame. This is because we have a measuring mark of perfection inside (although it's not necessarily accurate), and if we fall short of our internal mark of perfection, we have shame.

We want to get away from the mark of perfection and, instead, go for excellence or good. If you don't hit good, you don't have to have failure as the opposite reality. You can go back and rework whatever it is. Or you can come to the reality where you realize that you're not supposed to do it, you're not designed for that, and it's just not you to do it.

Don't Be Mean
to Yourself

*I*t's so easy to withdraw, to separate, and somehow to declare that as righteous. But that's a crime against yourself.

I often tell people, "Don't be mean to yourself," and they wonder what on earth I'm talking about. I'm talking about you withholding yourself from yourself. That's being mean.

Have no reasons that you can use to withhold your loving from yourself, no matter what. And that really means "no matter what."

Don't Lie to Yourself

*T*he Spirit has promised us that as we keep going forward to it, it will meet us and supply us—not necessarily to meet our greed, but to meet our need spiritually. And then we use our talents to bring that into the world.

Talents are those things that are creative and have Spirit in them. Your scheming and conniving come out of your lower self, and they have negativity and the Kal power in them. Don't kid yourself. Once you've lied to yourself, you can lie to the rest of the world with great ease. But you won't be able to live with yourself because you won't know who is lying to you, since if you'll lie to yourself, you'll surely think others will, also.

Innocence

The Bible says, "They brought young children to him that he should touch them. And his disciples rebuked those that brought them." In other words, they said, "Don't bother Jesus with kids."

"But when Jesus saw it, he was much displeased and said unto them, suffer the little children to come unto me and forbid them not. For such is the Kingdom of God."

What do children have? Innocence. And what do we have when we judge? Lack of innocence. So we continually have to come back to original innocence. And you can do that by forgiving and forgetting.

Seeing Through the
Eyes of Christ

*W*hen you practice seeing through the eyes of Christ, these are the first things that happen:

Judge not, lest you be judged. That's the first one. Don't judge. Whatever you see, you see it clearly, purely, as an experience, an expression for that Soul to evolve and grow— and that's exactly what it is. The Soul will evolve and grow, even in the most adverse situations. I've evolved more in adversity than I ever did out of blissful love.

The second thing is to forgive. No judgments—forgiveness.

And the third thing is to forget it. That's living right now in this moment of God's consciousness, in Christ that is in everybody.

Eternal Vigilance

*E*ternal vigilance is the password for forgiveness: the constant state of awareness where no harm is meant or intended for anything.

Know Yourself

ord Jesus said, "Forgive them, Father, for they know not what they do." But they all knew what they were doing: "We are killing this man who said, 'I am the light, the truth, the way.'" They went after him, stuck spears in his side, and put nails through him. And in the midst of all that, he said, "This I did for all of you."

And we sometimes think, "Sure you did. Why would you do it for me? You didn't even know me."

Jesus didn't have to know you. He knew himself. And that's the key: know yourself. Then you will be as Christ, and the mind that was in Jesus Christ will be in you—not as a crazy, radical, righteous person, where you beat people and say, "I'm doing this because God said I could," but more of the Shepherd tending your flock and making sure that if one gets caught in the brambles, you go after it and bring it back.

Any Time and Day

I think a lot of people have personalized Jesus Christ in very strange ways. I don't care to do that. I just know that he's the Lord of love. I know that God is love, and I know that if I stay in that as much as I possibly can, any time and day, I'm okay.

If I move out of that, I'm still striving to be back in that at any given time. I'm still okay; I just didn't have what was necessary to do it at a greater rate or level or percentage. That's all it says to me. But I don't condemn myself because I haven't been condemned. And I know that is so because I'm still being given opportunity.

The Greatness Is Inside

*W*e shut down God by moving into the world, professing God's greatness *out here*.

We've lost track that God is *inside* us in the greatness.

Regeneration

$\mathcal{W}$hen we talk about regeneration, we're talking about being whole spiritually, throughout our being.

If you do something, do it. If you don't, don't. Two minutes later, you don't remember what it was anyway. This is truly being born again, minute to minute.

If you keep staying in the past, then you're not a creature of regeneration; instead, you go to degeneration and start to die.

Whatever has happened in the past, with whomever, over whatever, is past. It is as simple as that because it's past. And whether they were right or they were wrong, whether you did it or you didn't do it, whether they did or they didn't—this is absolutely immaterial. I wouldn't even discuss it with you; I wouldn't waste my time to dignify garbage. And I suggest that you don't, either.

In God's Will

$\mathcal{T}$he Bible says that Jesus said, "When two or more are gathered in my name, there I am, also," and "What you agree upon, the Father will give you, if you ask in my name."

But he actually didn't say it quite like that. He said, "Where two or more of you are gathered in God's will and you ask of the Father in my name, keeping God's will present, I will give it to you."

Prayer

*W*e sometimes pray, "God, take away this. God, take away that. God, give me this."

But we never really pray the prayer that will truly be answered to glorify God, and that is to say, "God give me the strength to overcome all of these things and to reach into your glory and your kingdom." That's the prayer we need to make.

To Love, Honor,
and Respect

If we all could just honor and respect each other, none of us would have any history on us that we'd have to do anything with.

There would be no bad memories, no swear words, no yellings. Those would all be gone. There would be just this moment of honoring and respecting. It's almost like saying, "The Christ in me salutes the Christ in you." That's a wonderful thing to have.

A lot of you people have hurts inside of you because you wanted a certain thing, a certain way, and people wouldn't do it, so you felt hurt about it. You have a choice—to feel hurt about it or just drop it. If you're so smart and so intellectual and so spiritual, let's see if you have the wit to drop it. If you don't drop it, don't think you're so smart and so spiritual and so intellectual, because you're going to carry it as excess baggage, and that's not smart.

Open Your Heart and
Forgive Yourself

*O*pen your heart to Spirit and to all the hurt that you've experienced, and just say inside yourself, "I forgive myself for the mismanagements, misjudgments, misinformations, or whatever else has been happening that has made me feel hurtful, resentful, contracted, pulled away. I'm going to keep extending the loving again. And I'm going to keep expanding that, until one day it stays extended all by itself."

At that point, you're really going to be happy that you loved through the hurts and the discouragements and the despair and the crises, because you'll find out that it's really worth it.

The Days of Negative Publicity

I've gone through a lot of negative publicity, with people saying all sorts of things, and it's not even close to letting up. And I'm still loving and still going and still doing it.

I don't have any bad feelings towards any of those people who are negative towards me. At this point, I don't care to participate with them in what they're doing, but I imagine at some point in the future, I will. It's entirely conceivable to me that in the future, they'll be supplying great wealth and resources and love to the whole group. That's all inside of me as a possibility. And if it doesn't take place, there's no disappointment. Why? Because I've got the loving going.

You see, I put the people in a loving place inside of me, and I don't have anyone in there that I have a hurt, a hate, or an unforgiveness for. I will not do that to this temple of the Lord. I will not do that, because the Lord resides in here, Christ resides in here, and I will not defecate in my own temple.

The Days of
Negative Publicity

continued

That's what we do when we judge another. And we justify it through all the right reasons that seem so reasonable, except that they're all wrong. The only real reason is the loving and the caring and to keep cleaning up whatever gets dumped inside of you. And it's not easy. It's a daily task.

The Commandments

*O*ne of Jesus' great statements was when people came to him and said, "Lord, Lord," and he said, "You call me Lord, and it is true, I am your Lord, but why do you call me Lord if you do not do what I say?"

Many people turned and left Jesus at that point, because it was very easy for them to say, "Lord, Lord," and get what they wanted. But it was more difficult for them to say, "Lord, Lord," and to obey the commandments.

Yet the commandments are very easy: to love God with all your body, mind, and Soul and to love your neighbor as yourself. All the rest of the Bible is a commentary on that.

The Commandments

continued

There's nothing in there that says you can't make mistakes. Jesus said, "Judge not, lest ye be judged." And if you make a mistake, get busy correcting it, because he also said, "Don't talk about the board in somebody else's eye until you get the board out of your own eye." In other words, go around and perfect yourself before you start judging everybody else. After you've got that one out of your eye, you may realize that you've got other things to work on, so you don't get a chance to judge anybody else. You can say, instead, "I'm just so busy perfecting myself that I don't have time to know who's right and wrong."

You see, every time you judge, you hurt.

The Healing of the Day

*W*e can heal memories ourselves by going back in our mind and seeing where people did things to us that we didn't like.

We can ask ourselves what we would have wanted them to do and then, in our creative imagination, see them doing that new behavior. If there is still a residue, we do it again.

Is that a cop out? No, that's reality to heal the memory. Once it's healed, it's still there, but it's only a reference point. You haven't kidded yourself, but you're placing it so it does not control you or inflict on you. It is probably still there and probably still inflicting and still controlling, but not on you. You've healed it.

We can do this every night before we go to bed. We review the day. If a disturbance comes to mind, we see how we would like it to have taken place, and we envision it that way.

The Healing of the Day

continued

You'll get to the point where you lie in bed at night and ask yourself, "How was the day?" and you answer, "Fine. Good night." And then you get to the place where you get in bed, wake up the next morning, and say, "Wow, that was interesting. I wonder what yesterday was all about?"

Well, today is today. We get up and say, "Look at this day that God has made." And we don't wonder if it's going to be as good as yesterday because that means something in the memory needs to be healed. We let tomorrow go.

We have to forget things. The work of healing memories is a silent work. It's a work that goes on inside of you—how you love no matter what.

No Perfect Parents,
No Perfect Children

*W*e're here with what we've got, with what we know, with what we've got to work with, and there's no need to blame anybody, including our parents. What's amazing is, none of us had perfect parents. And none of our parents had perfect children.

When you look at that idea just through an intellectual approach, you can come back to yourself as a source of whatever is happening to you, and you can forgive yourself for not being the best that there is in the world. It's just a statement of forgiveness to the self, where you say, "I forgive myself for not seeing me being the best that there is in this world."

What Is
Forgiveness About?

*D*o you know what forgiveness is all about?

It's not about you forgiving me anything. It's about me forgiving me for giving myself over to the exterior senses and selling myself out and not having a wonderful, joyful life inside. That's the greater forgiveness.

If you forgive me, you've done yourself a wonderful favor, because I am no longer draining your energy (though I didn't know it). You're starting to pull in the energy that was being utilized in a very destructive, corrupted way towards you, and you're reclaiming it.

Doing What God Does

*W*hat you think, in your heart you're going to become.

Be careful what you think.

But if you think you are God, and you keep thinking that positive focus, guess what?

In your heart, you will become God.

And guess what you can't do then?

You can't do anything except what God does.

Relationships

*W*hen people talk about relationships, most of them say they want one. They say, "I want a beautiful relationship with a beautiful person, and we'll do all the beautiful things."

We say, "What would that person need to do to be in a beautiful relationship with you?" And strange as it may seem, they've got the answers: "I want them to do this and this and this and this and this."

We say, "*You* don't even do that," to which they reply, "I know. That's why I want *them* to do that. And if they aren't going do that, then I don't want them."

"Why don't you do it for yourself?"

"If I do it for myself, I don't need them."

"That's right, you don't need them. And here's a 'bombshell' for you: There's no relationship 'out there.' There's only a reflection of what you're doing inside yourself and how you're dealing with relationships inside yourself, not out there."

Self-Judgment

*S*elf-judgment is a terrible, terrible thing because it ejects the Christ inside.

The Key to the Kingdom

*S*elf-forgiveness is the key to the kingdom. It not only opens the door, it's the hinges on the door, it's the key to the door, and it's also the little bell that rings and lets you know the door opened.

Self-forgiveness is not an act of contrition or penance as much as it is a profound, radical approach to yourself. It cannot be mimicked, and you cannot pretend.

That's why it can help to get to the precision of it. If I hurt my mother's feelings and she is not here to apologize to, then I would forgive myself profoundly. I may say, "I would have liked her to be here, but since she is not, I forgive myself for any judgments I made on myself or my mother in that situation."

And then I would sit and let that forgiveness and the intent of it sink in. It often just goes "click" inside, and if you are doing this along with me, you may say, "Yes, that just let go."

No Blame

$\mathcal{W}$e need to come again to that place where we say to others, "I am taking total responsibility for myself and for my relationship with you and with anyone else inside of me. I do not blame you anymore for just being who you are because, truly, you are perfect. You don't have to change, and if you would like to change, that will also be okay."

What I must do inside myself is make sure that my relationship with you is up to date, present, and not based upon something that was happening last week or last month or last night or this morning, but is that which is present right now, here in my heart with you, so that I am here with you now.

The Mind of Christ

*I*n the Bible it says, "Let the mind be in you that is in Jesus the Christ."

That means to come to your own personal reality and have a direct relationship with your own Spirit. Be that. Have the direct relationship with God, and be that.

A State of Grace

A lot of the things we choose to keep remembering keep us stuck here on earth. Another option is for us to stay in a state of forgiveness, which is a state of grace.

Historically, we can see that those human beings who lived in the state of grace, as a statement of their lives, became the saints.

To live as a saint is to be living in grace and extending grace. Even when you want to tell somebody off, the words come out differently, and the person senses the grace you are extending to them, when you really had all the right, authority, and moral and ethical positions to have laid them low. When you withheld it, grace went in its place.

That's the forgiving that continues on, and you will not finish up the forgiving until your last breath.

Are You Crazy?

*I*f you base your loving of someone upon yourself, you will have already developed character and integrity—already developed it. And you will also have developed a certain loyalty to that place inside you where that person lives.

Relationships are difficult because most of the time we find the person's weakness and play on it. Relationships are set up precisely for us to practice on each other. Didn't you know that? Did you think it was to be perfect with each other? If you did, you are crazy!

Laughter

*T*here's one thing that works really well in this world, and I would suggest that you do this. Have a mirror by your bed when you wake up in the morning, and you pick it up first thing and take a look in it. Just take a look at who got up.

Then, at times during the day, walk into a restroom where there's a mirror, and just look at yourself and have a good laugh. And at night before you go to bed, take a look in that mirror and have another good laugh.

Don't forget to love yourself and laugh at yourself. In the midst of the most terrible, wrenching, insidious thing inside you, laugh. That's the time you need it the most. You have to get something to counterbalance the tremendous terrible thing, and laughter starts to bring it out so it can balance out.

If you don't feel like laughing, that's the time to laugh. If you've been practicing it, you can get it going. If not, pick up one of those mirrors and take a look.

It's All God's

*I*f you're really smart, you'll never attempt to own another human being.

If you're married to them, you have to remember that you're married to a partner of God and that they belong to God and you're just borrowing them for a while; you also have to remember that you belong to God.

That's what it boils down to. And if a child comes in, the child is also God's.

Your Inheritance

*W*hen we were born, every one of us was given a spiritual inheritance, and your name was written on yours. Before that policy becomes good, you've got to sign your name on the bottom so they know it's yours. And the way you sign your name is to go into the place where that policy is kept. It's kept inside of you, and it's called the kingdom of heaven.

You've got to go *in there*, disregarding everything that's said or done on this planet *out here*. You have to go past your hurt feelings, go past your victim consciousness, go past your mind, go past everything, and go in there just as purely as you can. That is difficult because to go inside saying, "Pure, pure," is not pure; it's a thought in your mind.

People ask, "Then how do I do it?" You make peace with yourself. You forgive yourself for all the things you've done where you know you didn't do the best you could. You say, "I did the best I could with what I knew, with what I had to work with." And that's it.

Your Inheritance

continued

The Bible says, "The evil of today is enough." You don't take it into tomorrow. So everything before this moment is past. You just say, "That's no longer real; it no longer exists. This is the moment that God has created, and in this day I have my life. And in this moment . . ."

With that attitude, you fall right back into the kingdom of heaven, and you get to find out that you're an heir to the kingdom.

Why Am I Here?

*J*udgments are one of the most unhealthy things we can do on all of our levels. If we were to ask what the big reason is that we're all back here, I'd say it was because of a judgment we placed somewhere, because our judgments are held against us, and they're held into the place where we judged.

So if we judge physically, the judgments are held physically, and we have to come back to clear them. But what do we do instead? We do more judgments.

It's enough to make you want to say, "Cut out my tongue before I do another judgment." Why? Because you are living your judgments now, so don't set up some more. If anything, when they come up, say, "I forgive that judgment."

If you do judge, the idea is not to beat yourself up or say, "I shouldn't judge myself," because that is also an action of judgment. Say instead, "I will be kind to myself. I will be good to myself. I will have peace and harmony with myself."

So What?

$\mathcal{T}$ake authority over yourself. Quit giving it away to memories, quit giving it away to childhood experiences, quit giving it away to interactions with parents or lovers or husbands or wives or whatever. Just quit giving it away.

Those things all happened. Yes, they happened. So what? Here is today. This is the moment where you say, "Yes, by God, those things were all part of my living."

You see, the choice is constantly in the mind, and it's one of choosing intellectually rather than emotionally. You don't do it as an irrational process but as a rational thought process. And it's this: If you think negatively, negativity is what you get. If you think positively, positivity is what you get.

So What?
continued

But what about this feeling you have? Make a joke of it. You go, "Ha ha ha," and then you suddenly ask, "Where did that feeling go?" It couldn't take the joke. It's a great ability to be able to laugh at yourself.

I wouldn't even dignify your past with any kind of response. Nor would I dignify my own or anybody else's. So you did it. So what?

Feeling Sorry
for Yourself

*A*s soon as that mean, ugly thing shows up in your mind, you usually say to it, "Why are you there? Did I put you there? Did I let you sneak in? Did you get in there because I wasn't watchful? Get out of here!"

Then you find that it won't go. Why? Because you must bring compassion into yourself; you must nurture yourself and kind of feel sorry for yourself. You actually sit down in a chair and say, "Oh, God, I didn't know what I did. I am really sorry that I did that, and now that I know, I do want changes."

It's a humbling of the self. Your pattern may not change right away. But when it starts up again, you challenge it once again, and in that challenge you once again strengthen yourself and empower the Divinity to come into you as a natural source of your energy, like breathing.

Call Forth the Christ

$\mathcal{W}$e cannot shirk the responsibility of always calling forth the Christ in everyone wherever we go. And we will only truly have the Christ awakened when we start to see it looking out of the eyes of everyone who looks at us.

God in All Beings

*Y*ou must forgive yourself all things.

You must have compassion for all people and the things they have done.

When you've done that, "you've done it to the least one of these; you've done it unto me."

When you've done it to "me," the Divinity makes itself known and floods the system.

We then see God in all beings, and we see the Divine in all things.

The Kingdom of Heaven

"Seek first the kingdom of heaven." And where on earth is that? Inside. Where inside? In its natural place of Divinity.

The kingdom of heaven is found in the place of your compassion. It's found in the place of your loving. It's found in the place of your generosity. It's found in the place of your healing of yourself and others. It's very easy to find the kingdom of heaven inside.

When we stop using the intellect of the mind and come to the wisdom of the heart, we access the door to Divinity, because out of that heart comes the compassion and forgiveness.

And you must first stand and forgive yourself for all things because it was ignorance that produced them in you. It was not Light. Christ himself said that he came into the world, but the world was full of darkness and didn't know the Light. So we forgive ourselves the darkness of our being and celebrate the Lightness that we are inheriting and that we're going towards, and we put Lightness into us.

The Kingdom of Heaven

continued

And when this body falls away, the Spirit-form that will be you will not have any of the personality things pulling on it.

So right now, pull up inside of you. Bless your exterior senses. Bless what you see. Bless the food you eat. Bless the bodies you touch. Be thankful for the clothing you have. Have compassion upon this planet; it's in need of it, but it can have compassion only from someone who carries compassion. *You* carry compassion. Exercise it through your senses, and you walk through it karmically free.

When Are We Forgiven?

*F*orgiveness looked at as a compassionate act must be looked at on the other side as a radical act.

When are we forgiven by God? When we do things God's way. Now that's a radical act. And when are we forgiven by Christ? When we come to Christ and become Christlike or do Christ's way.

The Question That
Deals With You

*H*e wins who endures to the end.

It doesn't matter what you think, what your lifestyle is, what you eat, what you drink—none of that. What matters is where you are going with your attitude and what thoughts you hold in your mind and consciousness. Where are you going with them? That's the question that you have to deal with. And that's the question that deals with you.

The Pure of Heart

"*B*lessed are the pure of heart, for they shall see God."

How do you become pure of heart? Do you go around thinking, "Pure, pure, pure, pure"? No, that won't do it.

There are two ways, and in both, you need to forgive. The first way is in your heart, where you forgive whatever you did that caused the upset. And the second way is "out there," where you forgive the other person for whatever they did. You may even have to forgive them that you knew them: "I forgive myself that I ever knew you, that you were my father, that you were my mother. I really forgive my bad choices. And I forgive your bad choices."

Then there's a third thing you have to do, and that's to forget it. The forgetting of it is the indicator of the forgiveness of it, and that is the indicator of the pureness of the heart.

This, Too, You Shall Do, and Even Greater

*I*t would be very foolish to have a Jesus Christ appear in a meridian of time and do all the things that we can't do, and then we go to hell because we can't do what he did. That has to be one of the dumbest approaches to any kind of game.

But he said a very interesting thing: "This that I do, you too shall do, and even greater because I go to the Father." If you're not doing the things that Jesus did, and even greater, what are you doing with your life?

If you're not forgiving your enemies seven times seventy, if you're not loving your neighbor as yourself, if you're not loving God with all your body, mind, and Soul—if none of that's being done, if none of that is true, if none of that's possible and you can't do that, then you can just put on a tin bill and go out and pick feed with the rest of the chickens, because it's of no avail to do anything else.

This, Too, You Shall Do,
and Even Greater

continued

And if it *is* true, then why aren't we getting to it? Maybe it's because someone left off some of the steps that have to be done. They forgot to say, "Through trial and tribulation do you learn the steps of creation. Through being hurt do you hold your hand back and not hurt somebody else."

And they also forgot to say, "This is a planet of trial and error and making mistakes." So get on with doing that so you can correct your errors, and then start to live a life of showing other people.

Letting Go of Shame

*S*hame is the worshipping of false idols. You worship your shame: "Oh, my God, I feel so ashamed. I'm so humiliated. I'm so depressed." And you worship those false things.

I'd like you to go into whatever places you have had shame stuck and take those false idols and cast them down. You just say, "No, I don't worship that anymore. That may come upon me, through whatever, and I'm just going to let it pass through and keep my eyes on the Lord."

It really is an affirmation: "I'm keeping my eyes on you, Lord, just you. I'm going to look at other people, but I'm keeping my eyes on you. I'm keeping the inner vision on you." When you do that, you may stumble and fall, but you don't know it; you get up and walk, and you weren't even hurt. But as soon as you focus upon where you fell and what hurt and what got twisted, that focus seems to be amplified by your consciousness until it becomes very, very painful.

Letting Go of Shame

continued

Take the thought with you that you're going to keep your eyes on the Lord. And if you're not sure where the Lord is, just keep looking, because he's there. He's always been there. And that's the neat thing about it.

The Tenderness
of Christ

I know that the Christ action will bring a tenderness to me that's like a fluffy cloud.

If you put your hand in a pail of water and you bring it out, the hole that's left is like the impression someone makes on me when the Christ is present. It doesn't stop anyone from putting their hand in it, but there's nothing that happens as a result of that.

So in a sense, in the Christ you're absolutely vulnerable and perfectly protected. And you learn to live in that because you're always having your going forth and your coming back within that. It's always there. When you go to sleep, when you wake up, it's always there.

Newness

*J*esus Christ was born in a manger, signifying that wherever we find ourselves, that's where we birth.

Right now, wherever you are, inside of you, you can start rebirthing, re-Christing.

In this, there must be innocence. To have innocence, there must be naïveté. To have naïveté, there must be forgetfulness. And to have forgetfulness, you must have forgiven.

And so we enter into the Christ action, which is forgiving, and we also forget. We enter into the awareness of newness and innocence, and, once again, Christ is born among us.

Speak Kind Words

*S*peak kind words, speak loving words, speak to the health and the direction of prosperity to everyone—not as a panacea, not as a Pollyanna approach, but as a divine truth that it is so.

Any negativity is just pointing out the next thing for us to work on and to bring across into the Divinity, until one day, and truthfully so, it will all be Divine, and we will know it as that. There will still be negativity, and there will still be positivity, and we will see it all equally as the Divine.

That is our heritage.

Baruch Bashan.

"And throughout all eternity
I forgive you,
you forgive me."

William Blake

About the Author

Since 1963, John-Roger has traveled all over the world, lecturing, teaching, and assisting people who want to create a life of greater health, happiness, peace, and prosperity and a greater awakening to the Spirit within. His humor and practical wisdom have benefited thousands and lightened many a heart.

In the course of this work, he has given over 5,000 seminars, many of which are televised nationally on "That Which Is." He has also written more than 35 books, including co-authoring two *New York Times* best-sellers.

The common thread throughout all John-Roger's work is loving, opening to the highest good of all, and the awareness that God is abundantly present and available.

If you've enjoyed this book, you may want to explore and delve more deeply into what John-Roger has shared about this subject and other related topics. See the bibliography for a selection of study materials. For an even wider selection of study materials and more information on John-Roger's teachings through MSIA, please contact us at:

MSIA®
P.O. Box 513935
Los Angeles, CA 90051-1935
(213) 737-4055
soul@msia.org
http://www.msia.org
http://www.forgive.org

Additional Study &
Resource Materials

An educator and minister by profession, John-Roger continues to transform the lives of many by educating them in the wisdom of the spiritual heart. If you've enjoyed this book, you may want to explore and delve more deeply into John-Roger's teachings through the Movement of Spiritual Inner Awareness. From among his vast body of work, we have selected the following for your consideration.

Soul Awareness Discourses–A Home Study Course for Your Spiritual Growth
The heart of John-Roger's teachings, Soul Awareness Discourses provide a structured and methodical approach to gaining greater awareness of ourselves and our relationship to the world and to God. Each year's study course contains twelve lessons, one for each month. Discourses offer a wealth of practical keys to more successful living. Even more, they provide keys to the greater spiritual knowledge and awareness of the Soul.
$100 one-year subscription
To order call MSIA at *323/737-4055*

Soul Awareness Tape Club Series
This audio tape-a-month club provides members with a new John-Roger talk every month on a variety of topics ranging from practical living to spiritual upliftment. In addition, members of the SAT Club may purchase previous SAT releases.
$100 one-year subscription
To order call MSIA at *323/737-4055*

Spiritual Warrior: The Art of Spiritual Living
by John-Roger
This book is essential for every person who wants to integrate his or her spiritual and material lives and make them both work. A practical guide to finding greater meaning in everyday life, this revolutionary approach puts us firmly on the higher road to health, wealth and happiness; prosperity, abundance and riches; loving, caring, sharing and touching. This book is a #1 *Los Angeles Times* Healthy Bestseller.
ISBN 0-914829-36-X $20 hardcover
Available in bookstores everywhere

The Tao of Spirit   by John-Roger
Eighty-one contemplative passages that can help you let go of this world and return to the stillness within. Timeless wisdom you can live by.
ISBN 0-914829-33-5 $15 hardcover
Available in bookstores everywhere

Walking With the Lord by John-Roger
A beautiful book about spiritual exercises—what they are, how to do them, and inspiration for your inner spiritual journey.
ISBN 0-914829-30-0 $12.50 softcover
Available in bookstores everywhere

The Way Out Book by John-Roger
A practical guide to spirituality—to living life more fully, learning from all your experiences, and becoming more aware of your spiritual nature. This book is packed with great and usable information.
ISBN 0-914829-23-8 $5 softcover
Available in bookstores everywhere

The Two Processes of the Mind:
Attitude and Altitude
An excellent introduction to the basic ideas of MSIA: checking things out, the levels of consciousness, spiritual exercises, moving beyond the mind to the wisdom of the Soul, and more.
$10 audiotape
To order call MSIA at *323/737-4055*

The Light, The Truth, and The Way
A classic seminar recorded by John-Roger in 1971, presenting the basic teachings of the Traveler.
$10 audiotape
To order call MISIA at *323/737-4055*

The New Day Herald
MSIA's own bi-monthly publication which contains articles by John-Roger and John Morton as well as other informative pieces and a listing of MSIA events around the world.
A one-year subscription is free upon request.
To order call MSIA at *323/737-4055*

Loving Each Day
A daily e-mail from MSIA containing an uplifting quote or passage from John-Roger or John Morton, intended to inspire the reader and give them pause to reflect on the Spirit within. *Loving Each Day* is available in three languages—English, Spanish, and French.
A subscription is free upon request.
To subscribe, please visit the web site www.msia. org

To order any of the items listed above, to learn about MSIA events in your local area, or to request a catalog for a wider selection of study materials, please contact MSIA.

MSIA®
P.O. Box 513935
Los Angeles, CA 90051-1935
323/737-4055
soul@msia.org
www.msia.org
www.forgive.org